Rip Currents

By Laura Townsend

Scott Foresman is an imprint of

PEARSON

Glenview, Illinois • Boston, Massachusetts • Chandler, Arizona • Upper Saddle River, New Jersey

Photographs

Every effort has been made to secure permission and provide appropriate credit for photographic material. The publisher deeply regrets any omission and pledges to correct errors called to its attention in subsequent editions.

Unless otherwise acknowledged, all photographs are the property of Pearson Education, Inc.

Photo locators denoted as follows: Top (T), Center (C), Bottom (B), Left (L), Right (R), Background (Bkgd)

Opener: ©Mike Greenslade/Alamy Images; **1** ©Giles Bracher/Alamy Images; **3** Jupiter Images; **4** Photolibrary Group, Inc.; **6** ©Dennis Decker/NOAA; **7** Visuals Unlimited/Corbis; **8** ©Giles Bracher/Alamy Images; **9** ©Mike Greenslade/Alamy Images; **10** ©Pixtal/SuperStock; **11** NOAA; **12** ©Andrew Palmer/Alamy; **13** ©Ed Taylor/Getty Images; **14** ©Epcot Images/Alamy; **15** ©Mike Greenslade/Alamy Images.

ISBN 13: 978-0-328-47284-0
ISBN 10:   0-328-47284-0

Copyright © by Pearson Education, Inc., or its affiliates. All rights reserved.
Printed in the United States of America. This publication is protected by copyright, and permission should be obtained from the publisher prior to any prohibited reproduction, storage in a retrieval system, or transmission in any form or by any means, electronic, mechanical, photocopying, recording, or likewise. For information regarding permissions, write to Pearson Curriculum Rights & Permissions, One Lake Street, Upper Saddle River, New Jersey 07458.

Pearson® is a trademark, in the U.S. and/or in other countries, of Pearson plc or its affiliates.
Scott Foresman® is a trademark, in the U.S. and/or in other countries, of Pearson Education, Inc., or its affiliates.

3 4 5 6 7 8 9 10 V010 13 12 11 10

Ah, a day at the beach! What could be more fun than sun, sand, and **surf**?

Watch out! Any beach with breaking waves can have a rip current. Rip currents are fast-moving sections of water that travel away from the beach. Some currents are narrow, but others can be 50 yards wide or more.

A day at the beach can be safe, or it can be deadly!

Rip currents travel along the water's surface, where swimmers are. Some beaches have rip currents all the time. Other beaches have them only now and then.

Rip currents can form around piers.

Often rip currents are most dangerous when waves are high and crowded together. Many times, rip currents are found at a break in a **sandbar**. They can also be found around piers.

When waves hit a sandbar, the force moves the water up and over the sandbar. But when those waves go back out, the sandbar blocks their flow.

Where does all that water go? It moves to a break in the sandbar, where it rushes back out to sea with lots of force. That force can create a rip current.

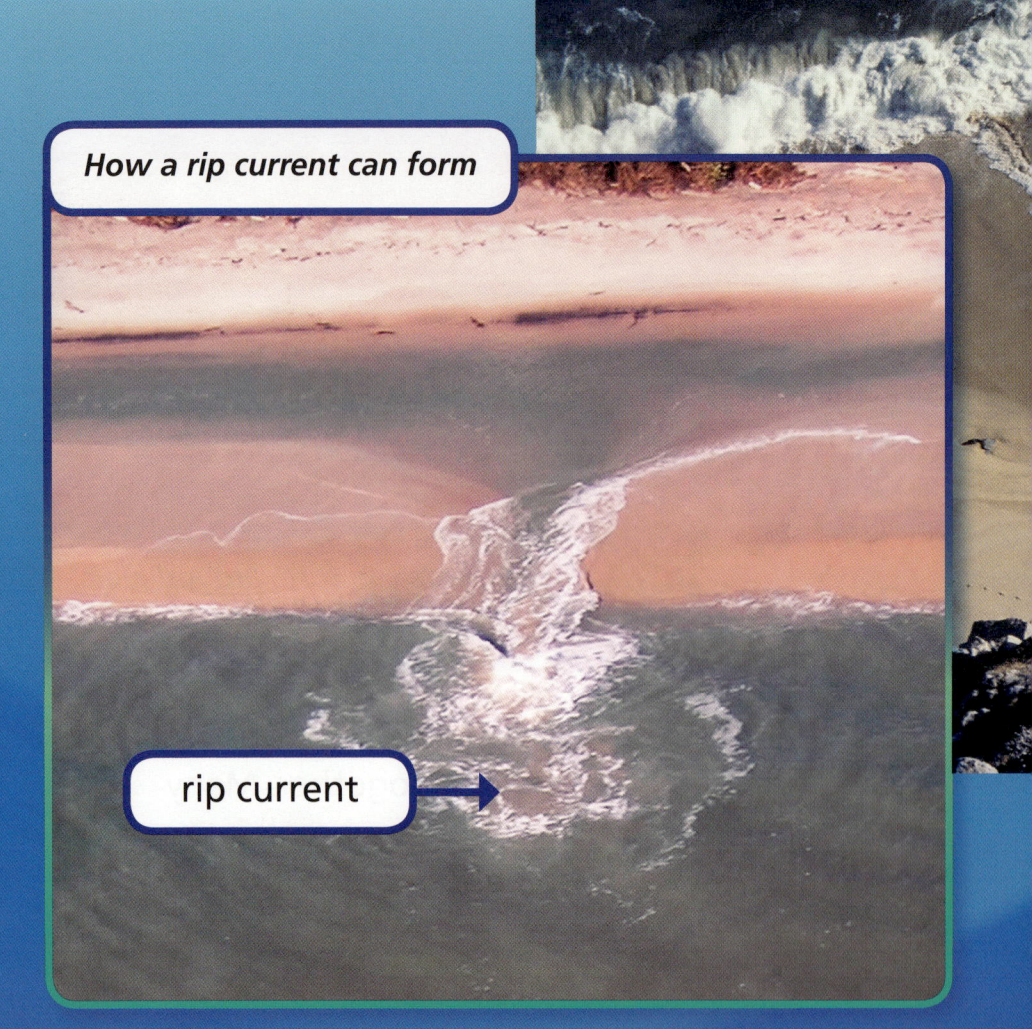

How a rip current can form

rip current →

Rip currents sometimes can be seen by swimmers. Sometimes they look like pools of choppy, **churning** water. When they carry foam, seaweed, or other **debris**, they look like a muddy river.

Rip currents can move as slowly as one or two feet per second or as fast as eight feet per second. That's faster than the fastest Olympic swimmer! Think how quickly that can carry a swimmer out to sea—even a strong swimmer.

All swimmers should know what to do if they get caught in a rip current. Lifeguards rescue more swimmers from rip currents than from any other dangerous situation. In the United States, as many as 100 people die every year in rip currents.

Why are rip currents so dangerous? They pull swimmers away from shore, sometimes very quickly. Even worse, swimmers may panic when they realize they cannot break free. When swimmers panic, they waste a lot of heat and energy, and they can't think clearly.

RIP CURRENTS
Break the Grip of the Rip!

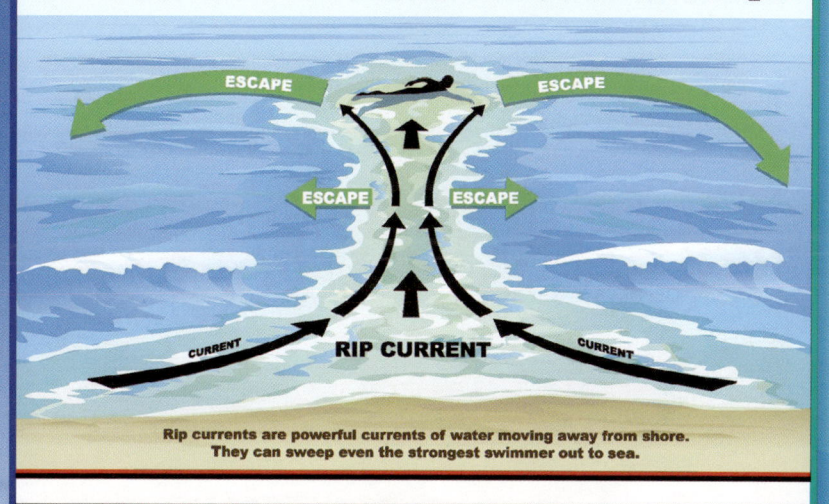

Rip currents are powerful currents of water moving away from shore. They can sweep even the strongest swimmer out to sea.

IF CAUGHT IN A RIP CURRENT
- Don't fight the current
- Swim out of the current, then to shore
- If you can't escape, float or tread water
- If you need help, call or wave for assistance

SAFETY
- Know how to swim
- Never swim alone
- If in doubt, don't go out

More information about rip currents can be found at the following web sites:
www.ripcurrents.noaa.gov
www.usla.org

If you're ever caught in a rip current, stay calm. Do *not* try to fight the current. Instead, swim **parallel** to, or alongside, the shore.

If you still can't escape, then float or tread water. Wait until help arrives or the current weakens. Call out or wave for help too.

If you see someone caught in a rip current, do *not* try to save that person yourself. Instead, tell the lifeguard right away. If you try to save the person, you might be carried out to sea too!

If possible, throw something that floats to the swimmer. This will help him or her stay afloat until help arrives. And always call 9-1-1 if more help is needed.

Remember these rules for a safe day at the beach:
- Know how to swim.
- Never swim alone.
- Always swim where there is a lifeguard.
- Follow all rules and signs.
- If you are unsure of the water conditions, stay onshore!

Smart swimmers are safe swimmers!

Glossary

churning *v.* turning around and around

debris *n.* left-over pieces of something broken

parallel *adj.* in the same direction as

sandbar *n.* a ridge of sand in the water, built up by currents

surf *n.* waves breaking onshore